Why I Live in TEXAS

101 Dang Good Reasons

Ellen Patrick

Copyright © 2005 Sweetwater Press

All rights reserved. No part of this book may be reproduced by any means whatsoever, neither mechanical, electronic, nor digital, without written permission from the publisher, except brief excerpts quoted for purpose of review.

ISBN 1-58173-398-4

Jacket and text design by Miles G. Parsons
Printed in Italy

1. If it can be done bigger or better, we'll do it.

2. We taught the world how to order a steak.

—⦻—

3. More friendly people per square mile.

4. It's too bad everybody can't be from Texas.

—∞—

5. You know that stuff in the tank of your car? You're welcome.

6. More famous musicians than any other state.

7. More famous writers than any other state.

8. More famous politicians than any other state.

9. More famous athletes than any other state.

10. This is where God lives. If you don't believe it, just look at all the churches.

11. Wang. If you don't know what it is, you ain't Texan.

# 12. Where there's Texas Red, there's fire.

13. Whistleberries.

---

14. We don't just live. We LIVE.

15. That rodeo state of mind.

16. Our cowboys throw both ropes and footballs.

—⋙—

17. Can you say "Longhorn"?

18. Are you a Republic like we are? Oh well, keep working on it.

19. Willie.

---

20. Lyle.

---

21. Le Anne.

22. More books written about us than any other state.

23. More movies made about us than any other state.

24. More songs written about us than any other state.

25. More TV shows made about us than any other state.

26. More winning teams than any other state.

—∞—

27. Only state that is tri-lingual (English, Spanish, and Texan).

28. You can have a multinational experience without ever leaving home.

———

29. The Hill Country in spring.

30. We could show other states how to fix barbecue if they would only let us.

31. Catfish-eating capital of the universe.

—∽—

32. Fishing so good you have to call 911.

33. Just a few little ole presidents from around here.

34. Shucks, we can't help being so great.

35. Ruby Reds. Widely imitated, never matched.

---

36. Mockingbirds in spring.

37. Desert sunsets.

—⌁—

38. Rockets know how to fire off a basketball.

39. Astros know how to shoot for the stars.

—∞—

40. Lyndon and Ladybird.

41. Birthplace of German chocolate cake.

—∞—

42. Cock-a-doodle-moo.

43. If you can't find it in Dallas, it doesn't exist.

44. We have lift-off!

―∞―

45. People in other states watch TV. We just look out the window.

46. If it was good enough for Jim Bowie, it's good enough for me.

47. We gave the world Dr. Pepper.

—⋙—

48. We gave the world corn bread and beans.

49. We gave the world the picante experience.

50. Dale Evans.
You go girl.

51. Farrah.

---

52. Waylon.

---

53. Buck.

54. T-Bone.

—⚬—

55. Lefty.

—⚬—

56. Jerry Jeff.

57. Kris.

—⚡—

58. Flaco.

—⚡—

59. Howard Hughes.

60. Cadzilla.

61. If Red Adair cain't put it out, it cain't be put out.

62. If you aren't eccentric, you aren't normal.

---

63. There's a word for what we got here. It's called gusto.

64. Golfing that borders on the religious.

65. Hunting that borders on the religious.

66. Fishing that borders on the religious.

67. Shopping that borders on the religious.

68. You can ride an elevator in the morning and ride a horse at night.

69. Texans make the best neighbors.

—⚘—

70. Texans make the best friends.

71. Texans make the best relatives.

72. Texans make the best chili.

—⁂—

73. Largest state fair in the U.S.

74. Tyler roses in October.

---

75. Hard to say which we have more of: black-eyed peas or bluebonnets.

76. Onions so sweet it can be embarrassing.

—∞—

77. Where else would you find the hushpuppy Olympics?

78. Polka music induces unlawful levels of frivolity.

79. Square dancing threatening to wipe out depression and anxiety.

80. If you get bored, you can always round up some rattlesnakes.

81. Gators outnumber people in some places.

—⋙—

82. Only state where the cowboys are real.

83. Only state where cowboys also write poetry.

84. We learn how to ride horses. Then we learn how to walk.

85. We ain't afraid to fight.

---

86. We ain't afraid to win.

87. We ain't afraid to lose, but we will go down kickin'.

88. Even hurricanes think twice before hitting Texas.

89. If you are afraid of produce bigger than your head, you won't like it here.

90. The San Antonio riverwalk on a summer night.

—⚡—

91. The Dallas skyline on a winter morning.

92. Houston humidity in August eliminates need for expensive saunas.

93. Padre Island beaches eliminate need for tranquilizer prescriptions.

94. Winter influx of snowbirds improves mental health of entire nation.

95. We don't mind sharing <u>Austin City Limits</u> outside the Austin city limits.

96. We are simply not afraid of overeating.

—⁂—

97. We have little or no difficulty with self-esteem.

98. Where else can you rope a cow in the morning and dance in high heels at night?

99. We can live without water, but not without sweet tea.

---

100. A beer now and then never hurt anything either.

101. You can leave Texas, but you'll always come home again.